TAU

April 20

That which does not kill us makes us stronger.

✧ Friedrich Nietzsche ✧

LILY

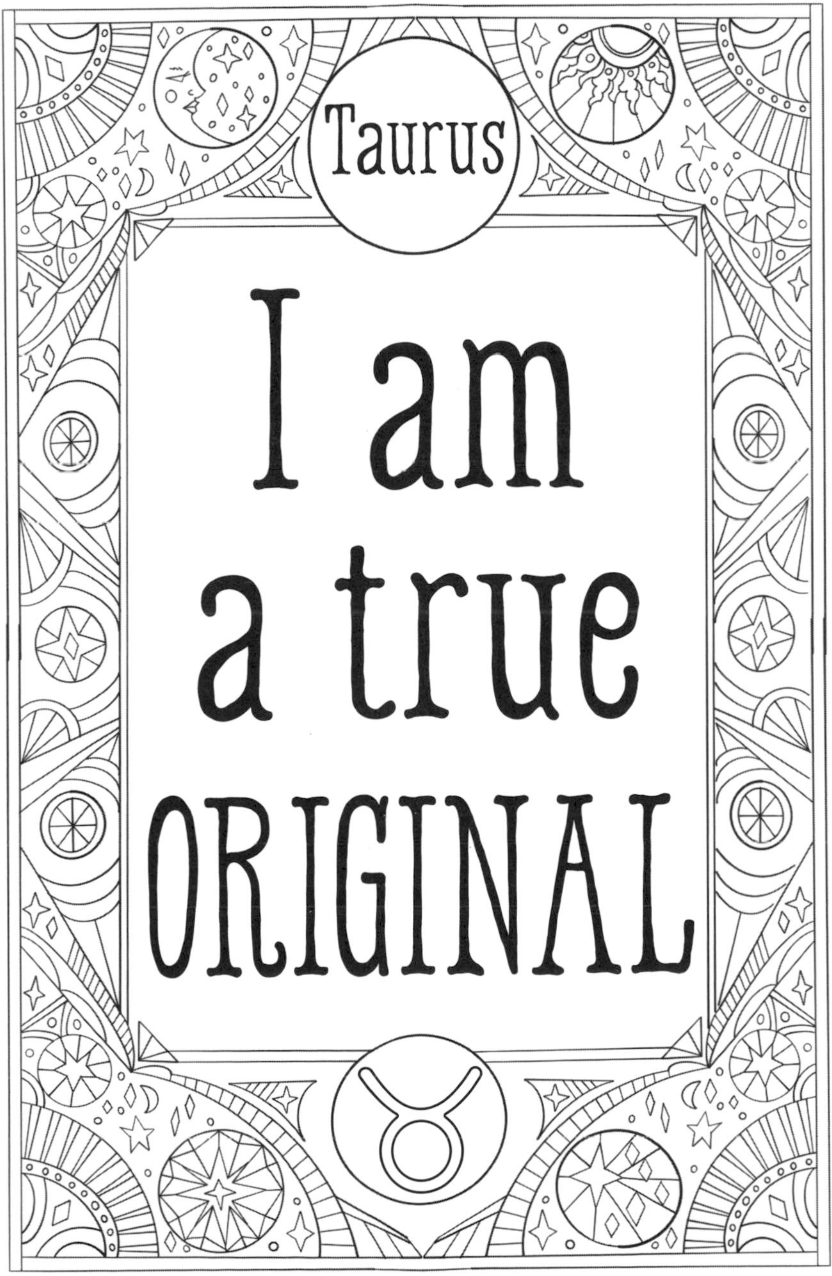
Taurus
I am
a true
ORIGINAL

spring

Taurus

Taurus
Ruled by Venus

Taurus

Creative

DETERMINED

Loving

TOUGH

LOYAL

RULING HOUSE 2
The House of Value

TAURUS

My work makes a true difference

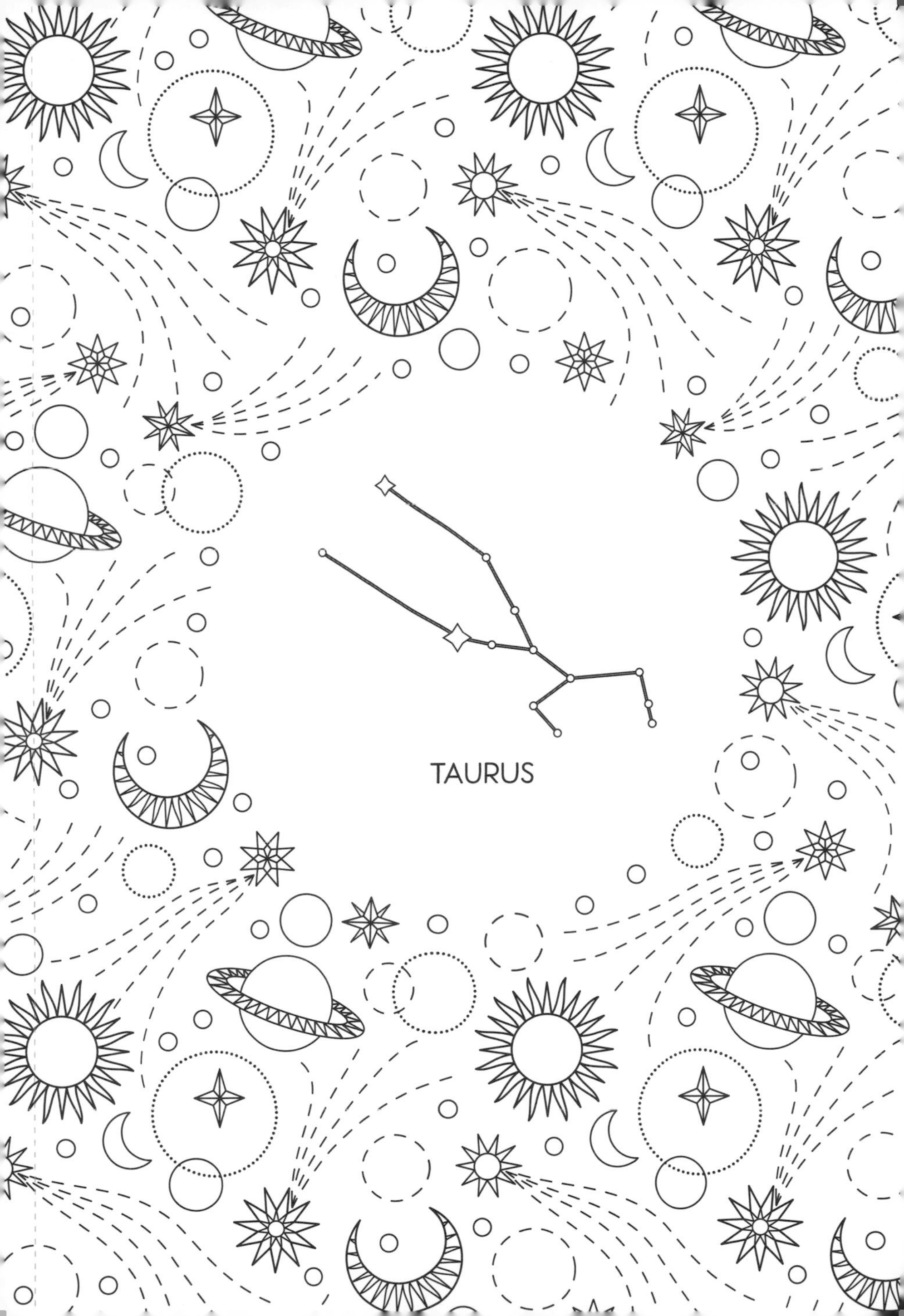
TAURUS

Aries
Taurus
Gemini
Cancer
Leo
Virgo
Libra
Scorpio
Sagittarius
Capricorn
Aquarius
Pisces

Earth Signs
Taurus
Virgo
Capricorn

LET THE STARS LEAD THE WAY